My Testimony

"Behold I give you power and authority"
(Luke 10:19)

By
NORMA RODRIGUEZ

1

About the book

My Testimony By Norma Rodriguez Founder, Jesus Saves International Ministries

This book is more than a personal journey. It is an invitation to encounter the transforming power of God. Through these pages, I believe readers will be challenged to rise to a higher place of faith, step into a deeper relationship with God, and experience the healing, hope, and restoration that only His presence can bring.

As someone who once walked a path of brokenness, I know what it feels like to be lost, lonely, and without purpose. I was a little girl burdened by pain and hopelessness, trapped in cycles of depression, alcohol abuse, and generational bondage. Everything changed when Jesus Christ came into my life 26 years ago. He took my sin and shame to the cross, set me free, and began a work of transformation that continues to this day.In this book, I share testimonies, my own and those of others, whose lives were miraculously touched by the power of God. From prison cells to juvenile detention centers, I have witnessed firsthand how the Gospel breaks chains and restores purpose to those who felt beyond saving. What once felt like a mess, God turned into a message of faith, redemption, and unconditional love.

If you have ever felt like a nobody, let this be the story that reminds you that in Christ, you are somebody. A life without direction can become a life filled with destiny. Through His grace, we are made new.

To God be all the glory.

About the Author

Norma Rodriguez was born and raised in the heart of Houston, Texas, one of twelve siblings in a home marked by hardship and brokenness. Emerging from a life shaped by poverty, family struggles, and the pain of a fractured home, Norma encountered a life-changing moment in 1986 when Jesus Christ called her out of despair and into a future filled with hope and purpose.

Today, Norma is a licensed minister and the founder of Jesus Saves International Ministries, passionately committed to sharing the Gospel with those in need of redemption. She brings a message of healing, salvation, and transformation to prisons, communities, and nations, offering light where there once was darkness.

Her life is a living testimony of God's grace. Through this book, one of her proudest accomplishments, she continues her mission to preach the Good News, make disciples, and help others find the same hope that changed her life forever.

TABLE OF CONTENT

CHAPTER ONE 8

MY FIRST LOVE 8

CHAPTER TWO 14

THE BACKSLIDDEN YEARS 14

CHAPTER THREE 22

COMING BACK TO MY FIRST LOVE 22

CHAPTER FOUR 26

MY INTIMATE MOMENTS 26

CHAPTER FIVE 34

FIGHT THE GOOD FIGHT OF FAITH 34

CHAPTER SIX 42

MY CALLING 42

CHAPTER SEVEN 52

CALLED OUT 52

Dedication: To my number one fan, my mother. I will always be thankful for your love and support as you gave your life for us all, just like our Lord and Savior Jesus Christ. You will always have a lasting memory in my life with the Lord. Thank you for all your prayers.

To my children: Cheli Rae, Malerie, Jessica & David.

Thank you Lord Jesus for the privilege to write to those who through this book will read and see that You are all they will ever need. I also thank you for those who will read and see through this book that you are life to those who accept you.

To my family in the Lord whom has been an inspiration in my walk with the Lord, thank you for your prayers and encouragement and support. May His blessings and angels encamp you always.

Acknowledgement: Jesse Rodriguez, for dedicating your life as a husband and father as you provided and served the Lord and our Country in the Armed Forces of America.

Betty Jean and Richard Money with Christ the Healer Evangelic Ministries, I will always cherish the memories in the work of the ministry together as we did door-to- door evangelism, hospital ministry, fed the homeless downtown and the Bible studies in your home. You are true warriors, soldiers and pioneers for our Lord. And of course, the Power Evangelism School of Ministry—I wouldn't be who I am today without your help and support; thanks for your dedication.

Geno Kelly: A true Warrior for the Lord. Thanks for your support and your dedication in the word and for being a good friend; you have been an iron-sharpens-iron kind of friend. Thank you for your boldness—keep Preaching the Word, friend!

Houston Revival Center: Pastor LA Rue Adkinson, thanks for your deep teachings as you fed the sheep solid food for our growth in Jesus and continue the great work in Building God's Kingdom for such a time as this.

To Carolyn Clark: God divinely connected us to venture me out into my ministry. I thank God for you and your friendship and for all of the open doors that He has brought my way—thank you foryour encouragement and support.

CHAPTER ONE

MY FIRST LOVE

Growing up in the inner city, the heart of downtown Houston, life was empty and I was not sure that anything good would come out of it. I was the seventh born to my mother and father, who had twelve children together: eight daughters and four sons.

While I was growing up, school was the only good thing in my life. There was no religion of any sort in my upbringing. By the time I reached six years of age, my mom and dad had divorced. After their divorce, my mother became both a mother and father to us all. She was unable to work, so as a result, we had to live on government help for many years. My life was filled with divorce and alcohol abuse, which became my example. Children learn from what they see and I was evidence of that.

I never had guidance, encouragement or emotional support as a child and while growing up I felt like I was lost in my big family. By the time I was eight years old, my best friend and I found ourselves across the street from her home in a little church called Calvary Mission Baptist Church and every day after school it became home to us. This church also housed

homeless people and the Reverend overseeing it was like a father to my best friend and I. God rest his soul. I can recall every week after service that he'd take us to the neighborhood store to buy our favorite candy, pop, chips and his favorite drink, Tab.

We were close to different families around the church.Brother Manuel was the assistant pastor there and one night—I was about nine or ten, a very young girl—he was doing the service and I remember him saying that they were going to pray for someone and cast out a spirit, and if anyone in the service was not saved they were to leave the sanctuary. The choir was made up of two of Brother Manuel's daughters, my best friend, and myself. The organist was Brother Ray. He had a problem with one of his legs, but he sure could play a good ole hymn. We were invited to sing at some event and the Reverend wanted us to be a uniformed choir. I couldn't go home and ask my mother for money as we were low on income. Looking back, I see how God was ordering my path.

Reverend decided to buy our dresses and shoes. It was exciting to me because I never had anything new growing up. We continued to serve the Lord there by cooking meals for the families. We went to the market to buy vegetables, eggs, and produce to feed the people. These families were from all walks of life. I was fortunate enough to have my own home, so the church became my second home. We were established there in that location for about a year and a half. Later the church moved to a different location, so I left with the church without my mother's permission. The people were moved to an apartment complex temporary. Later, I heard that my mom was looking for me, and she sent for me. As I was on my way to her, I felt as if I were leaving my family, people that I was really close to. I felt as if the home I was going to was my adoptive home.

When I walked into the small two-bedroom home, my

sister informed my mother that I was back. She asked where I had been; I told her all the things we had been doing with the church and all. She didn't pay much attention, but was relieved that I was back home. Soon things were looking up for the church and the church found a new place to worship—the old mission across the street from my best friend's home was desolate and shut down.

The new church location was about four miles from home and at times my friend and I took the bus when we couldn't wait for the Reverend to pick us up. The church had eventually settled in and began to have services again. Our first Christmas there was warm and happy. I came home with presents for my own tree and God had been good to us.

As time went on it was hard to keep the church functioning. Brother Manuel had a hard time in his personal life, which really affected his ministry as an assistant Pastor and he was threatening to kill himself. Across the street from the church one night, he was waving a weapon of some sort in his hand as we looked on from a distance. I didn't have all the details but I believe he committed suicide. Soon the church was closed and the families were relocated. I felt like all I ever lived for was over. No more choir to sing in, no more church to go to and no more services to hear the word. But God never left me; my church days were not over yet.

CHAPTER TWO

THE BACKSLIDDEN YEARS

The next nine years of my life were the hardest. I went in a different direction since the church was closed. I smoked my first cigarette when I was eleven years old and had my first drink at twelve years old. At thirteen years old I experimented with marijuana and harder drugs. I went to Mexican dances with my friend and her family and things went downhill for me from then on. I left home and moved away with a man eight years older than me. I thought it was the best thing that could have happened to me. We moved away from Houston to a small town in East Texas, in a small duplex apartment. I was only fifteen. I had a baby by the time I was eighteen. I considered an abortion but couldn't go through with it. I was even more depressed and drank more for the pain. I was overwhelmed with the thought of a new baby when I couldn't take care of myself.

I found a job down the street from the house to keep busy, but that didn't fulfill me. I needed to go back home to start off new and go back to school, but that didn't happen. I stayed and got more depressed. One day while I was cooking dinner and cutting meat and had a knife in my hand, suddenly I had a thought come to me in my weakest moment that said, "If you just did this, you wouldn't be in all this pain." That devil was making a suggestion for me to kill myself! The devil is a liar as I see now how he comes to kill, steal and destroy. I snapped and realized that it wasn't right. I thought about my baby and how her life would be without her mother; she was only about six months old. Two young men lived next door and I believe they were Christians. I was at work one day when they came in to visit with some of the workers there and heard them talking to them about religion and about the coming of Christ.

We moved into a home to have more room after the baby was born—a nice two-bedroom home. It was comfortable to live there, very peaceful and lots of shady trees. An older couple that lived next door to the duplex at the time called me after we were settled in the new house. They invited me to the church one Sunday. I accepted. I remember going out the night before; we went out with friends to a country club. We came in late that night and I had to get up early that morning to get to church with my neighbor. I didn't want to let them down.

I struggled to get up and get dressed with the baby. I had no idea that the Lord was dealing with me. My husband was outside painting the house. I left that morning with a big hangover. I was at this little church all hung over and barely able to keep myself focused on the service. I don't remember the religion. I remember going to alter for prayer and nothing much happened. I didn't feel different. I was just hung over and ready to go home and get back to bed.

I missed my family in Houston, as I was not used to a small town. The baby's dad and I were not getting along and things grew worse. I didn't know how to get myself together. All I knew while growing up was drinking and going out all hours of the night, and to think I was only eleven and twelve years old already hanging out in bars and clubs when I should have been at home in a safe place and at school. I was looking for love in all the wrong places; the relationship with my child's dad didn't last.

I moved back home to Houston, moved in with my

mom, looked for work and tried to make it on my own. I did not make good choices. I remember going downtown on a cold sunny day in January 1985. I walked into a Mexican restaurant to apply for a waitress job. The next day about 2 p.m., I received a call from the manager for an interview and he was satisfied and hired me. I got a job as a waitress. I look back and see how God was divinely connecting me to this man. He was a kind and generous man. He extended his generosity to my own family; as I look back, I see how this man was so much like a Boaz in the book of Ruth and I couldn't see it at the time because of the blinders in my eyes. God was bringing restoration to me and doing a good thing in my life. We were married sooner than later. We went on a honeymoon to Hawaii. My future was looking brighter as I worked as a waitress downtown for the family business. My neighbor who lived across the street knocked on my door one day and shared the gospel with me. She opened to the book of John. I wasn't a Christian yet so I didn't understand what she was doing.

When she left my house that day, I remember closing

the door behind her and as I peeked through the peephole I saw her dancing on the way out. I believe that the Lord had made a pact for my life that day. Later that day, I felt something warm come all over me, like a blanket. It's the only way I can describe it. God used this dear sister to lead me to Him that day and my journey began. Looking back I see how God blessed me with a Boaz like in the book of Ruth. God divinely connected Ruth with Boaz as Boaz married Ruth and was kind and generous to her. Ruth 2:13 & 4:13. I became pregnant and had a baby girl in October 1986 and another baby girl in September 1987.

By this time I received a call with bad news: my little sister, who have turned 19 years of age on November 9, had committed suicide on November 5, 1986. The devil was going about as a roaring lion seeking whom he may devour. He was working on one of my brothers to destroy his life as well. My family was all converting to Christianity and the devil hated it. My brother lost his best friend during all this confusion. His best friend died in his arms. It was on the local news. The word was out that my brother was being held as a hostage inside the house where the incident occurred. The SWAT team was there to arrest the suspect; news later reported that my brother was downtown giving testimony on the incident. My mother was also recently saved and baptized, and she prayed hard for all her kids from then on.

We held Bible studies at homes and fellowship with each other as much as we could. I was longing to be part of a church.I tried a couple of fellowships with my neighbor in people's homes; later I tried the Catholic Church, but it didn't satisfy me. About two years passed and we moved from the south side of Houston to the northwest side of town. I stayed home and raised my daughters. By this time they were one and two years old, and I decided to take care of the children in the neighborhood to have extra income. My next- door neighbor invited me to come to a little Baptist church one day and much to my surprise, I found that God was getting ready to bring me back to Him.

CHAPTER THREE

COMING BACK TO MY FIRST

LOVE

I remember going with my neighbor to church that Wednesday night and later leaving full of joy as we had been filled with a Holy Laughter. I can't explain it, but to this day I know it was the Lord. We went to the convenience store that night. We bought the kids candy, chips and pop. Much to my surprise, the Lord had reminded me how we used to go the store after church when I was a little girl with my best friend and the Reverend. We could not stop laughing that night—it was awesome!

That next Sunday I visited the church for Sunday services. I remember walking in that morning with a hangover. I felt bad inside and out. That April Sunday morning, I heard the choir sing. They sounded so heavenly. I went home that day and went back on a weekly basis. I became a member in the summer of 1988. I got baptized and was never the same. I got involved in the children's ministry children's choir, children's missions and child care and did vacation Bible school every year, as well as mission trips to

Chihuahua, Mexico.

A choir member approached me one day and invited me to join the choir. I was reluctant at first and later joined. I was coming back to where I used to be many years ago. The enemy thought that this soul was lost and destroyed forever. He tried his best, but his best was not good enough.

I stayed in the church, learned the word and had lots of fellowship with the people. But as time went on I found something was missing—the Holy Ghost! Signs and wonders, prophesy, tongues, gifts of healing and so on. Why did they stop at salvation? I struggled to stay there many years, praying that God would move mightily as I waited and prayed a glimpse of revival was at the threshold. I went to get more of God in other churches where all the word was taught and gifts were practiced.

CHAPTER FOUR

MY INTIMATE MOMENTS

In the early years of my Christian walk, about 1995–96, there was a man used mightily in the healing ministry. I watched his programs for many months on TV. I heard he was coming to the Coliseum in our town. I was so hungry for the Word, so I made plans to go. When I got to the meeting I could feel the presence of God all around. There were people in lines waiting to get in; people came from other churches and others were there to be healed. I went to get filled with the Living waters Jesus offers to all who thirst. I came home so blessed that night and as I read the word, I saw how Jesus told His disciples that the same power that He had, He gave them that would believe. Guess what? I believed, and I used that same authority as Jesus in the Bible. I was praying for the sick and exercising my gifts everywhere I went. I prayed for people in parking lots, at Walmart or any department store I went to just to exercise the gifts.

Back to the event, the doors would not open until 7

that evening.

We arrived two hours early so we could have good seats. It was like having church in one big auditorium. We would have fellowship with other believers and sing songs to pass the time. Finally the moment had come. I felt as if I was going on a date. I was ready to be with the Lord. He was all I desired in my life. I had a longing desire to know Him.

The service began with an hour of worship and praise. Sometimes the flow of the spirit would go for an extra hour the man of God would be under the anointing. He would give a message on healing and would close with worship and praise; the Holy Spirit would begin to heal the sick and the hurting.Many miracles took place at each service.

Zechariah 4:6 says, "It's not by might nor by power, but by My Spirit, saith the Lord of Hosts."

It was an awesome experience. I read all the healing scriptures and tried to memorize them. This transformed my life and I was never the same. I was drawn in the healing ministry. I practiced laying hands on my own children when they were sick and the Lord would touch them each time. I bought some books on the healing power of God and found how the Lord had healed many people and heard how God was a compassionate and merciful God, and this made me want to touch people like Jesus did in the Bible. It seemed that the more compassion I had, the more God worked through me.

I began to see through His eyes how people were in bondage to all kinds of spirits. I had a hunger to see people healed and set free through the power of the Holy Ghost. I feasted on the Word on a daily basis. I didn't want any distraction while I was in the Word. He was all that mattered to me. I remember a story of a man coming to the disciples to have them cast a demon out of his son. The story goes on to say that they were unable to do the job. They asked Jesus why they couldn't cast the demon out and Jesus replied saying, "This sort of thing can only be done through prayer and fasting." So Jesus had to cast the devil out. Mark 9:14-29. I practiced fasting and praying and saw signs and wonders. This day and age we confess Jesus as Savior and Lord, but we have no idea of why He came. He came to save that which was lost. Matthew 18:11. He didn't come for those who were well, but for those that were sick. I found that His love for me was so amazing that He would lay down His life for me (John 15:13). The Bible also says that many are called and few are chosen. God was preparing me for a great work. I could not resist the call. God's Spirit was hovering to find someone He could use. His voice calls those He chooses. The Holy Ghost does all the work, if you believe all things are possible and God backs up his word.

And I heard the voice of the Lord say, "Whom shall I send and whom will go for us? Then I said, here am I send me" (Isaiah 6:8). Are we ready to take that call on in our lives?

It is God's will for you to be healed. Mark 1:41 shows how Jesus feels about our sickness. Mark 9:23 also shows us that you will receive what you believe. If you've never experienced the supernatural work of the Holy Ghost, this would not make sense to you. The SUPERNATURAL is unexplainable; that is why it's called a MIRACLE—this means God did it and receives all the glory. Most people don't believe, for the religious have never been taught about miracles. Jesus said miracles were done so that the lost might believe. If you're a Christian and don't accept the word regarding miracles, you are not accepting all of Jesus and His word declares; if anyone is ashamed of Him and His sayings, He too would be ashamed of you (MARK 8:38).

I continued to go to the meetings every time the man of God would come. I wanted to know all the works of the Holy Ghost. I wanted God to use me in this area of ministry. It was awesome; I didn't want to come home. I could feel the presence of God all around me, even to the next day, and it was an intangible feeling. I had a desire to see the supernatural work of God in the church. I was filled and had to use all I learned. But I had grieved the Holy Ghost for fear of what the people at the church would think. All the other churches I visited were in agreement with the power of Holy Ghost. The pastor at my church did not teach on the gifts and such, but I couldn't keep quiet too long. They had to know there was a God who still heals people.

I continued to go to church and felt out of place. I did my best to fit in, but to no avail. It was impossible. The Church was established in a conservative neighborhood. I thought of leaving but I guess God was trying to establish my life with a good foundation because the Pastor did preach a lot on the family. I made lots of new friends and got close to many families. I used to be loud and bold in the world and the church I attended didn't have people of my kind there. I was just representing the one I used to serve when I was in the world. In the Bible this is called "rebellion," a form of witchcraft. Now I was on God's side, so I had to learn to represent Him.

CHAPTER FIVE

FIGHT THE GOOD FIGHT OF

FAITH

I was now in the army of God and had to learn to put on the whole armour of God to stand against the fiery darts of the devil (Ephesians 6:17 & 20). I heard someone say that the only thing the devil knows how to do is throw darts at us, but he can't touch us because we have the sword of the spirit. Everyone knows that a sword is bigger than a dart, that the sword is the Word of God. I learned to speak in Truth and with Boldness every time. The devil came to tempt me but I reminded him about the Word of God. This was the only way to get him off my back. The devil comes in all shapes and forms. You will learn to recognize him by being in the Word of God. He comes in opposition to the Word of God each time. So, stay in the Word and be ready, child of God. If I came across any problems in my own life, with finances, for example, and I began to worry, all of a sudden the Spirit of God would arise in me and remind me my God shall supply all my needs according to His riches in glory (Philippians 4:19). When sickness was knocking on my door, I came back with the Word that says, "I am the God that healeth thee" (Exodus 15:26), and another one that says, "I will take sickness from the midst of thee"(Exodus 23:25). Then I would shut the door on the devil's face. You see, what the devil tries to do is check to see if you have the Word of God in you, and he tries to convince us that the Word of God is not true. If you don't know the Word is really true, then you will also doubt His Word. When the devil came to tempt Jesus, guess what Jesus did? He quoted the Word of God each time. I went to church faithfully with my two daughters. The pastor believed in the family and how God intended for the family to live. I guess you could say he believed in family values and the responsibility of the parents to the children and so forth. In 1994, God opened doors for me to teach a Bible study in Spanish at the Apartment Ministry our church was involved with. I never expected to see and hear all the great things God would do there. We were able to minister to mostly Hispanic families. The two ladies from the church taught English as Second Language and I did the Bible study. I was reluctant at first because my Spanish was not the Spanish they spoke. Eventually I went and did the best I could. I had no knowledge of teaching a Bible study; this was a challenge to me. The lady from my church gave me a little book to teach out of. Ironically, it was on the ministry of Jesus— on how Jesus went about doing good to all and healing all that were oppressed by the devil, casting out devils and feeding the multitudes. It was awesome! This was confirmation that I was on the right path and God was getting ready to do a great work and prove to many that He still heals and performs miracles signs and wonders. This was what we were called to do—Church! No matter what religion, if you desire to be like Jesus, this is what we ought to be doing. We are to walk like Him and talk like Him. Lay hands on the sick that they might recover. It was through miracles that many came to Jesus and followed Him (Romans 15:18-19). Miracles were done for those who didn't believe in Jesus, who were once gentiles and later became believers. If you believe, you'll receive when you pray (Matthew 21:22).

We met in one of the ladies' apartments for weekly Bible studies. There was a young lady who came to the Bible studies a couple of times. She was about five months into a pregnancy. One week, she did not attend the Bible and we got word that she'd been rushed to the hospital because she was hemorrhaging. She had a history of losing her babies at about this stage in her pregnancy. We prayed for her that day during the Bible study and the following week we got word that she was at home doing much better. The bleeding had stopped.

The lady went on to have her baby full-term and God gave her the desire of her heart: a healthy baby girl with no further complications. Another lady had asked for prayer for her son who had severe asthma attacks and could hardly go out to play with the other children. She came back with reports that the boy was doing better after prayer and was able to play with the others once again. When one of the ladies heard about what God was doing, we prayed for her daughter who had been complaining about pain in her ears; she had to have tubes put in her ears, but to no avail—the problem was still there. She came back with news that her daughter was healed and was pain-free. Hallelujah! The same lady asked for prayer for her husband who had a drinking problem. She gave testimony that her husband had cut down on his drinking! Testimonies are a vital part of a Christian's life. When the unbeliever hears, they have an option to Believe and receive their Miracle. In Romans Paul says that many believe through the Miracles (Roman15: 18-19).

Testimonies will cause others to have Faith to Believe to Receive. The Bible declares that Faith Comes by Hearing and Hearing by the word of God. (Rom. 10:17). The ladies had the faith when they heard the testimonies; therefore they received. The same week a lady asked for prayer for her son who was picked up from school earlier that morning due to fever. She said every time he got this way the fever would stay for three to four days at a time. We prayed for him and the following day the child was off to school. Reports like this will build people's faith. The Bible declares that without Faith it's Impossible to Please God (Heb 11:6). There was a lady that we prayed for after the Bible Study. We were asked to come to her and pray because she was going to into labor too early about her eight month. We were told that her neighbor downstairswould be delivering her baby soon. That day, when we prayed for her, the pain went away and she was able to hold on to have her baby at full term. Praise be to God! Many other miracles were done that are not mentioned in this book.

CHAPTER SIX

<u>MY CALLING</u>

In spring 95, we had a three-day Revival at the Baptist Church. I had been at church longing to see and feel the presence and power of God. A lady I knew personally had come to us for prayer before the service began. She was a worker with children's ministry. We assured her we would lift her up in prayer and she went back to her job with the children. I did not feel led to pray for her there and then, because I was afraid of how the people would receive that. I been going through a battle with the devil and deciding whether or not to stay in the church. So I had once again grieved the Holy Ghost because of what people would think. As the service began, we were worshipping through songs with my hands lifted up. All of a sudden I felt the Holy Ghost lift me up, off that pew to pray for this lady. I went about looking for her. When I saw her she had her eyes fixed on me, I called her out of the room that she was in with other workers. I told her I needed to pray for her and that God was going to heal her. I had no choice. God would not leave me alone. God told me if I didn't go to her she would end up in a wheelchair. She led me to a room where we would not be interrupted. There were two doors on each side. As we walked in she immediately locked the doors, the presence of God was already there. To do the work and ready to heal this lady, she sat down and began to tell me her situation. She said she had gone to the doctors for excruciating pain she had on her ankles. They were also becoming weak, which made her unable to hardly walk. The doctors thought it could be Lupus or some other form of crippling disease. She shared with me later how her husband had to carry her into the house due to her illness. This was a healthy forty-five or fifty year old. She shared how the doctors could not find out what her problem was and what the diagnosis could be. When I shared with her the goodness of God, she began to weep. The presence of God was all over the room. I taught her the scriptures where God's word declared. He was The God that healed and the other that God said He wanted to heal us and she believed and was miraculously healed. I remember being in the kitchen the next day as I prepared dinner early in the afternoon. I received a phone call about three o'clock. It was the lady I prayed for the day before. She said after we prayed she was healed and got her strength back on her legs and feet and she was no longer in pain. Hallelujah! I was so encouraged and full of God and continued to minister to the sick and the hurting. This is the work that God commands us to do church (Luke 9:1-2). The bible says, "These signs shall follow them that believe; in my name they will cast out devils... they will lay hands on the sick and they shall recover!" Mark 16:17-18.

Now I knew I had a calling to minister to the sick. The bible declares God has put these in the church: prophets, evangelists, teachers, and administrators. Some to perform miracles and healings! The devil did not like the reports and was trying to get me out the church. All this is going on while we were having a three-day revival. The next night this same lady came. She walked in to the sanctuary as service began. She was still weeping. The power of God was all over her. Right before the service was about to begin, she was asked to come up to share what God had done for her. She began to share but could hardly contain herself as Gods presence was still all over her. I could feel rejection in the midst. I know how Jesus must have felt when in His own people rejected Him. You could've heard a pin drop. The Holy Ghost was working on others to come forward for their miracle while she gave her testimony. A lady in the congregation who was our bible study teacher came forward as she heard the testimonies and grabbed my hand and rushed us to the altar. She shared how doctors recently found a lump on her breast. We prayed that night at the altar and the following day she called me and told me the lump had disappeared by the time she got home.Hallelujah! A lot of people are taught to get saved, to receive Jesus and to live a good Holy life. But they are not taught about the gifts. He wants you to use it. He does not want you to be ignorant church. It's all or nothing-- the same power Jesus has, we have-- and in Jesus name we have the authority to use it.

I remember when Jesus said, "because of their unbelief, He could do no great works there". The devil does not like this in church, that's why Jesus was chased out each time. The enemy brought lies into the people's minds and a lot of whispering was going on. I would feel the tension rise of what they were thinking. I got a call from the lady I prayed for and "the word" was that the leadership didn't want this to get out of hand; they feared the church could go in the wrong direction. I remember in the book of Acts how the leaders did the same thing as they held a meeting to stop Peter and John from spreading the signs and wonders they performed in

Jesus Name. Acts 4:13-17. They were ordinary men and uneducated. Guess what? I was a candidate for the call -- I qualified!! I felt like Jesus did when He read the scripture that said, "Today this scripture is fulfilled in your hearing" (Luke 4:21). I remember reading this same passage in the teacher's class (lady with the tumor) one day as she asked me to share. God was stretching me for greater things. People didn't believe Jesus was the Son of God. Jesus was chastised and chased from His own town. I didn't let the devil get the best of me so I stayed a little longer. I was called a witch for performing miracles and accused of getting paid for healing the sick. They didn't realize that they were wounding their very own. These were my friends in the Lord. I fellowshipped with them, sang with them, did ministry with them and now asked to leave by the pastor. He claimed they didn't believe that way and that I should not mention his suggestion about my leaving to anyone. I eventually found refuge in another church for about a year. I went back to reconcile with the people and thought that God would use me there once again- and He did. I had been back to the church, when one day after the service I was walking to my car and I could feel the Holy Ghost guiding me in a particular direction. I couldn't understand it. So I just followed His leading. I saw a group of kids pushing a little girl in her wheelchair. I knew God was up to something. There must have been about eight or ten children around her. I walked towards her and found she was one of the twin girls my daughter played with in church. She had an identical twin and I could not tell them a part. I asked her parents what the problem was with her. They said she had been to the doctors and her hip joint was deteriorating and they said she would not be able to walk on her own for a long time. The only thing they could do was to give her medication. I asked if I could pray for her, they agreed. I looked down at her as she sat on her wheel-chair and I asked her "would you like Jesus to heal you?" she looked up to me as if seeing Jesus and she lifted up her hands. She smiled at me and I asked all the children around to agree with me. We prayed and went on our way. Two weeks later, I was at church on a Wednesday night and saw all the little children running in the gym. I saw one of the twins running and thinking it was the other twin. When all of the sudden the two were running together, one of them was the little girl we prayed for. Her parents said they took her to the doctor visit and the doctors declared her healed. The doctors called it a miracle. Hallelujah! A lady at one of our bible studies at the church was trying to have a baby and was unable to conceive. I was led to go to her at some point during the bible study and encouraged her to read the passage where God said He would open the womb of your belly and bless it. A few days passed and as I walking into the ladies room when all of sudden she and another lady said to me, we have something to share with you. Her friend seemed to have been shaken over the miracle. She was literally shaking as she spoke to me as she was leaning against the wall. The lady that conceived was coming out of the dormitory and began to say that she was going to have a baby. She believed and conceived and we rejoiced together and gave glory to God! And later when we were going to have a concert at the church, we were sitting around at the dinner table. As everyone ate before the choir went on to sing, a young lady was talking about not being able to have a baby, I went onto say to her that God would bless her if she believed His word. We prayed for her and she conceived and had a baby nine months later. HALLELUAH!!!

We had a concert with the choir on another occasion at the church. I was asked along with another brother to share our testimonies.

He would do his in English and I would do it in Spanish. As most of the audience would be Spanish, I agreed and worried that others that would come would not understand as I shared in Spanish. God gave me wisdom at the last moment and as I began to share. I gave my testimony in Spanish and English. I shared on how I was lost without God and how I drank to relieve myself of depression and how God had delivered me and my family of alcohol and drugs and that He would do the same for those who gave their lives over to Him. God was good that day and many came forward as God was already dealing with them as they heard our testimony. Many tears were seen as I remember sharing and when the minister gave the invitation they came forward and were prayed for and others counseled to receive Christ. About fifty plus came and were touched and healed as they heard and believed. About two weeks later, we were at choir practice on a Wednesday night and the director had shared that he received phone calls from those that came. Two of them in particular were healed physically. They had been back to the doctor and doctors could not find anything wrong regarding their illness. They reported that God had healed them that night. Hallelujah! God is good to us!

CHAPTER SEVEN

<u>CALLED OUT</u>

Therefore come out from among them and be ye separate, says the Lord! Notice there had to be a separation to be called 2 Corinthians 6:17. God called the Apostle Paul minister to the Corinthians to come out of darkness. He will cleanse you and use you for your Calling. I was going through a transition in my life about the future regarding things I had not accomplished. I believe now that the devil was trying to get me off track and cause me to miss my "Calling," as I was praying on the things in my heart. I thought about going back to school. I made phone calls and met with the counselors to register. I always wanted to be in the medical field to care for people with their sicknesses and pain. I waited and the time was not right then. Much to my surprise, God had a plan on how I would be doing that. I didn't know which way to go on the decisions. I met a couple through one of the members from the church. She was doing outreaches with them. She shared with me about their ministry. I learned that they were evangelists. I found out they lived right around the corner from me and I was interested in what they did. I offered to help them establish their ministry through their home. I received their monthly bulletin and found they were going to be having a school on evangelism. I got excited and gave them a call about the school, especially because it said, "Free school" on the bulletin. She shared and gave information and next thing I knew I was attending their school. (Power Evangelism School.) We did a thirteen-week course of extensive ministry on a weekly basis. We fed the homeless downtown on Tuesday nights. We did Friday night Bible study in the ministry, door-to-door Evangelism on Saturday mornings, church on Sunday. After church services we did hospital ministry. I remember going out on our first outreach on a Tuesday night. I was learning to minister outside the four walls of the church. We were directed to go in two's to pray with people. A man approached me and my partner. He smelled really bad and had alcohol on his breath. But God helped us overlook all these things. The man began to share about his life. We prayed for a long period of time with this particular man. He shared on how he had received Jesus in prison and that he was having a hard time being a Christian out here in the world. We encouraged him to get into a good Bible based church, where he could grow in the word and learn to resist all the temptation the devil would throw at him. He would weep and kneel to pray repeatedly and later he exclaimed with a shout. We asked him what happened to him. He told us "I could see!" He went on to say the Lord gave him his sight back—Hallelujah to Jesus! He didn't speak English too well. My partner wanted to know what the man was sharing with me. He told me to tell her the Miracle so I told her all he had said. He shared that he had just gotten out of prison for killing someone and that he was staying with a friend in the downtown area. He forgot his bi-focal eyeglasses at the apartment and didn't need them anymore because he was able to see clearly-Hallelujah!!

We rejoiced with him and he asked prayer for a friend because he had glaucoma. We left there overwhelmed at all the things God had done through His people. At the end of our course we were to go to Mexico for one week. The pastors handed out information about it and I was reluctant to sign up due to the lack of my finances. So I left it in the Lord's hands. Later I was asked to come on the Mexico trip by the lady that did the ministry. She shared how they needed someone to speak Spanish with their group to translate for them when they preached down there. I told her I was unable to go because of my financial situation. The trip was going to be about seven hundred dollars. She said that they would pay my way and that all I had to do was come. Hallelujah! We went to C.D, Victoria in Mexico about a twelve-hour drive from Houston. The Lord even blessed us with one of the couple as they took their R.V. We had room to sleep on the way with a kitchen and bathroom, T.V and VCR. God was good to us. We had a joyous time on the way. I remember getting there that night that cool spring 1998 and the pastor ran up to R.V. and opened the door and rushed us out to come, as it was time for us to minister that night. The meeting was to begin and as we were introduced to the people that night I could feel an expectation in the midst. I knew God would do something great. The people were ready to receive. They were hungry for what God had for them - the pastor was from India. He shared how God moved in his heart to go to Mexico and preach the Gospel. He was to sell all he had and go. They lived in Pasadena Texas, a small town on the outskirts of Houston. His wife was a registered nurse. He left for Mexico to find where God would establish him with only his black little pickup truck. When he got there, he later awoke from his sleep and said, as he looked around he saw a lot of need there for ministry. Poverty and a lot of religion and idols surrounded it. God told him that was where he was to build the ministry. They sold all they had and went off to Mexico. They went and had help from other churches from all over the country. He now has a place called Casa De Esperanza meaning (house of hope). Churches come to his aid to evangelize, to preach, to teach, to do vacation Bible school and build up the church. They stay for as long as one month to one year whatever time the Lord puts in their hearts. God had blessed the meetings we had every night. As we were getting ready to leave I had a desire to return. We kept in touch through letters and phone calls. I was able to see the missionary and his wife when they came to Houston for business or when they came to visit other churches to share about the ministry and all the good things God was doing there.

I went through with the school, and to my surprise found out that we would be receiving diplomas as we graduated. I was able to get licensed by the State of Texas. I was able to bring all we had learned into the church I attended. We fed the homeless on a monthly basis in the downtown area. We had a group that helped out faithfully. It was a blessing to see the ministry grow and all the volunteers the Lord brought to support the ministry. We fed anywhere from one hundred to one hundred and fifty men and women on the streets and parks of downtown Houston. Many prayed to receive Jesus and filled with the Holy Ghost. With the evidence in speaking with new tongues, I was amazed to see how God would heal and set many free from bondages. Later the church I attended adopted the homeless ministry and set up a budget for our monthly expenses. God was preparing the church for the work of evangelism in this area of ministry.

People in church pray for a move of God or Revival. But Revival begins within our hearts and spending time in the word. God desires for these gifts in all churches. That's how Revival comes to the church when one person takes a stand and stands in faith and truth and demonstrates His power. The Name of Jesus is able to heal deliver & set the captive free from all bondages. Jesus said, "I am the way the truth and the life he is the gift God freely gave" (Romans 6:22-23). If you have never made the decision to receive Jesus as Savior and lord consider making that decision today. Tomorrow is promised to no man. Pray to receive Jesus by praying a simple prayer, "Dear Jesus, I repent of my sins. I ask you to come into my life and be my savior and lord. I believe you are the Son of God and God raised him from the dead. I will follow you and tell others about you in Jesus name" amen.

Congratulations you have made the most important decision of your life!!! You have crossed over from darkness to light. You are a new creature in Christ (2 Corinthians 5:17). Your name is written in the lamb's book of life and you are now registered for heaven. Find a church that teaches all of God's word. It's important that you read the bible and get connected and stay active in a church. Stay in fellowship with other believers. Tell others about your New Life in Christ and how all your past has been washed away because of Jesus. Jesus has come in to make you new. Jesus was not ashamed to die for us therefore we should not be ashamed to tell others about Him. Pray always and seek him as you follow him and he will direct your path.

Conclusion

Jesus gave us the word to grow as Christians. To help us in the direction we need to go. Jesus said, "you shall know the truth and the truth shall set you free" when you buy a car, you get a manual book to know the car and get familiar with it to help you know how to care for your vehicle. It's the same with God's word, it instructs us how to live for him and follow the path he has for us.

When you buy a product you also get instructions to use that product. So it is with the bible. God will show you how to live a life pleasing to Him, it will take time as with a new born baby. That baby will not grow until time has gone by then it becomes an older mature person.

As you stay in the word, you will get wisdom and understanding and mature in Christ. You will drink milk for awhile like a new born and then begin to eat table food just like an older toddler afterwards becoming more mature into a teen and so forth. So it is with growing in God. It will all depend on the time you spend with the father in his word. To God be all the glory for the great things he has done!!

"They overcame him by the blood
of the lamb and the word of
their testimony"

(Revelation 12:11 KJV)

Notes/ Prayer request

www.ingramcontent.com/pod-product-compliance
Lightning Source LLC
LaVergne TN
LVHW051202080426
835508LV00021B/2767